Rookie
Read-About® Science

The Solar System

By Carmen Bredeson

Consultants
Dr. Orsola De Marco
Department of Astrophysics
American Museum of Natural History
New York, New York

Katy Kane
Educational Consultant

Jeanne Clidas, Ph.D.
National Literacy Consultant

SCHOLASTIC INC.
New York Toronto London Auckland Sydney
Mexico City New Delhi Hong Kong Buenos Aires

Designer: Herman Adler Design
Photo Researcher: Caroline Anderson
The photo on the cover shows the solar system.

ISBN 0-516-24492-2

12 11 10 9 8 7 6   6 7 8 9/0

Printed in Mexico.   61

First Scholastic paperback printing, February 2004

Did you know that our big, bright Sun has a family? The Sun's family is called the solar system.

Planets and their moons travel around the Sun. So do asteroids, meteoroids, and comets. They are all part of the solar system.

Asteroids and meteoroids are space rocks. Some asteroids are as big as a mountain.

Meteoroids are smaller than asteroids. They can be as small as a grain of sand.

Asteroid

A comet is like a big snowball with a rock in the middle.

Comets start to melt when they get close to the Sun. A melting comet has a long tail.

Planets are an important part of the solar system. Nine planets go around the Sun.

Mercury

Venus

Earth

Mars

The four planets closest to the Sun are called rocky planets. Mercury, Venus, Earth, and Mars are made of rock.

Mars is the red planet. Iron in the soil gives Mars a red color. Many space probes have visited Mars.

Jupiter

Saturn

Uranus

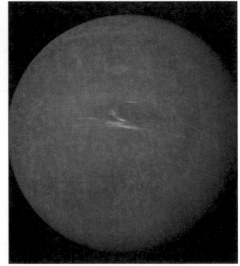

Neptune

The next four planets are called gas giants. Jupiter, Saturn, Uranus, and Neptune are made of gas.

You could not stand on them. It would be like trying to stand on a cloud.

Saturn has beautiful rings around it. The rings are made of pieces of ice. Some of the pieces are as big as a house!

The farthest known planet in the solar system is Pluto. It is smaller than Earth's moon. Pluto is solid like the rocky planets.

There are many moons in the solar system. Most of the planets have at least one moon. Only Mercury and Venus have no moons at all.

Moons of Saturn

Earth has one moon.

Jupiter has thirty-nine moons!

On Earth, we have air
to breathe and water to
drink. Crops grow in the
warm sunshine. Earth is
just right for living things.

The night sky is full of lights. Most of the lights are stars like our Sun. Some of those stars have planets.

Could there be another planet like Earth?

Words You Know

asteroid

moons

comet

planets

30

solar system

space probe

Index

About the Author

Carmen Bredeson has written dozens of nonfiction books for children. She lives in Texas and enjoys traveling and doing research for her books.

Photo Credits